MORE MISERY
THAN JOY

John Burke

Order this book online at www.trafford.com
or email orders@trafford.com

Most Trafford titles are also available at major online book retailers.

Printed in the United States of America.

ISBN: 978-1-4269-3719-4 (sc)
ISBN: 978-1-426-93720-0 (e)

*Our mission is to efficiently provide the world's finest, most
comprehensive book publishing service, enabling every author to
experience success. To find out how to publish your book, your way, and
have it available worldwide, visit us online at www.trafford.com*

Trafford rev. 7/21/2010

 www.trafford.com

North America & international
toll-free: 1 888 232 4444 (USA & Canada)
phone: 250 383 6864 ♦ fax: 812 355 4082

This book is dedicated to:
Tarja Hannele (Hienonen) Burke
My Darling wife (passed away March 22, 2009)

And to Norma Dakin, who said to me:
"You should at least publish one book!"

A BETTER DAY

Mama, Papa, My dear Sis,
I am left alone in this great abyss,
And I am tired of being all alone,
And I am seeking that eternal place,
Where Angels dwell, and see God's face,
The Place that is to be our final home!

And, I don't think He meant me harm,
But into His ever loving arms
God, now took my loving wife,
But He left me here, on this earth.
And took away all my mirth,
To live out my remaining, empty life.

How sad it is, that I feel;
Tell me. Is this truly real?
Is it right to be crying all the time?
What was it that I did, to deserve all this?
What fateful lips did I kiss?
Tell me now, please; what it is, that was my
crime?

Love my fellow man, you say,
And this is the only way,
To lift from me, this cursed curse!
But it's difficult, don't you see?

My fellow man does not love me.
He's never done so, since my birth!

So I guess, I am, without a doubt,
The only one I care about!
Selfish yes; rightly, you may conclude.
But in the space I am in today,
I can never seem to find a way.
Please excuse me, for being rude.
Tomorrow may be a better day!

THERE'S A NEW DAY A COMIN'

There's a new day a comin'
There's a new day, and it's not far away.
There's a new day a comin';
Listen to what I say!

No more laughter,
No more tears!
No more sweating out those
Lonely years.

There's not much time
To say goodbye.
A big grey bomb is fallin'
From the sky!

So long, goodbye,
God help us,
Prepare to die.
So long:
Hello Bomb!

ANGEL

This is the night I longed for,
A night of heavenly bliss,
To hold you closely, in my arms,
Your lovely lips to kiss.

This is the night I dreamed of,
For many, so many a day,
To gaze into your beautiful eyes,
And "I love you" will softly say.

This is the time I longed for,
To finally make you mine.
This is the hope I hoped for,
For such a long, long time.

And even though I love you,
I know that you must go,
But I hope that soon, you'll be back,
I truly do pray so.

But while you're gone, please think of me,
And in a longing way,
For I am always thinking of you,
Each and every day.

So, my darling; my Angel,
Believe me when I say,
My love for you, is very true,
I'll love you for always!

BACKWARDS

I go to sleep in the morning,
And I wake up late at night,
I just can't seem to do
Anything right.

Going down to the ocean,
Hand hanging on my head,
I've got things to do,
Down at the ocean's bed.

Davey Jones' Locker was waiting there for me,
I went down just to see what I could see,
I woke up in the hospital,
With a terrible fright,
I just can't seem to do, anything right!

Maybe I should start turning things around,
Try to fly, when I want to stay on the ground,
Do you suppose this
System's sound?

CALVARY

So here I am,
So forlorn;
Through life's highway
I must tread.
My limbs are weak,
My eyes are dim,
And I feel the dread,

Is it something that is haunting me?
Is it only in my head?
Or is there something coming?
Something closing in?
Is it my own delusion?
Or is it my mortal sin?

When I meet my Maker,
What is it I will say?
Will I cry for mercy?
Or take what comes my way?
Oh, God, how I long to be,
Placed within your Joy,
But I am an old man now,
Not a little boy.

My faith, it has diminished,
As the years went passing by,
I long to get to Heaven,
But, all I do is cry.
For the suffering of the world I cry,
Surely; I'm not to blame!
I had no big part in it.
And that is my solemn claim!

But we all know the answer,
So very plain to see,
We were the very ones,
That put Him there!
Put Him on Calvary!

CHEATER

Your sweater is inside out,
Your underwear, worn backward,
Have you been somewhere I don't know?
There is no need to answer!

You've been cheating, you can't fool me!
I've known it from the start,
But I love you, Baby, way too much,
Although it breaks my heart!

Yes I'm a fool, there is no doubt,
A fool I've been, but maybe,
Sometime in the future,
We could work things out, My Baby

Tell me what I must do,
To win your love for me?
But maybe it is way too late.
Whatever is to be?

I'm tired of all your lies,
Pretending that I don't know,
I'm sick of it, and someday soon,
I will let you go!

CHICKENS

Chicken? Chicken? What a funny word!
Who thought to name it quite like that?
I think it's quite absurd!
After all, everyone knows, it is just a bird.

Chicken? Chicken? It can be cooked,
In so many different ways,
Am I being bold?
But Colonel Sanders has the best,
His secrets, never told.

Eleven different herbs and spices,
He would not reveal to me!
But I would be happy if I, if I,
Could find that recipe!

It would save me money,
It would make me glad,
If I only knew the secret,
And the money that he had!

So now, I should be satisfied,
With the things that I do know.
In the morning, I will boil,
A chicken's embryo!

CRAZY, AM I?

Some people say that I am peculiar,
In a funny way,
That I am a little left of center,
An eccentric, is what they say!

That I am one brick, short of a brick load,
That my elevator doesn't go straight to the top,
That I have bats in the belfry,
These compliments just do not stop.

That I am as crazy as a bag of hammers,
Not the sharpest knife in the drawer,
And maybe it's true, I must admit,
I've heard it all before!

So let us get straight to the point,
Some people say that I'm insane.
Let us decide for sure,
By playing a little game.

Let's pretend that I am the hunter,
And that you are the prey,
Ready or not; here I come,
I hope that you can pray!

It's all a game, can't you see?
Nothing I said is true!
Don't worry now, all is well,
I'm not really out to get you!!

But can you really be sure?
Ha, ha; ha.ha.ha!

CREATIVITY

They say that Creativity,
Is the offspring of Pain,
That art, it would diminish,
If happiness were to reign.

Well, I don't know if that is true,
I didn't put it to the test.
For happiness is so far from me,
I have no gauge, I guess.

For all I know, it maybe false,
Some poems do spring from joy.
But joy, I never experienced,
Since I was a boy.

The saddest part about it is,
That in the dark of night,
I wake up crying from all this joy
And I begin to write.

Nothing witty, nothing smart,
Nothing to amuse the mind.
And sometimes I get so tired of this,
But nothing else, can I find!

To ease the pain and suffering,
I just keep writing on,
Until I meet my Maker,
The heartache won't be gone.

I'm sorry to inform you,
I must truly say,
That Art and Poetry will live on,
Until the Earth passes away!

DESTINY

I feel that I'm an empty vessel.
Only fit for the potter's shards!
Tossed and thrown upon the rivers,
A destination lost and marred.

A rescuer, I cannot see,
Between here and eternity,
I'm bound and chained, without a hope,
A darkness for my destiny!

The chaff I am, and not the wheat,
Nothing ahead, but defeat.
Whoever can endure until the end?
I'm telling you, it's not me, my friend!

I'm in the throes of despair,
I see darkness waiting there!
Should I pray to God above?
And beg for His Eternal Love?

But I'm not worthy: So many sins.
I'm afraid to turn to Him.
To be rejected, I could not bear,
I guess I'm trapped in Satan's lair!

And this is the condemnation, that light is come into the world,
and men loved darkness rather than light, because their deeds were evil.
For every one that doeth evil hateth the light,
neither cometh to the light, lest his deeds should be reproved.

John 3:19, 20.   K.J.V.

DISTANCES

Just sitting in my misery,
The one I love;
So far from me.
If I could open her eyes
That she could see,
Just what it is.
She's done to me!

But that? It just can't happen,
Not within my power,
So I just long for her, with a sigh,
Each and every hour.
Every hour that passes by,
Makes life a little dour.

What is it that I lack?
That turns love away from me?
What is missing? What did I do?
Or is it my personality?
It starts out great, but in the end,
It is the end of me!

GOD, GRANT US WISDOM

God, grant us wisdom every night,
And through the day time, too,
Just for a second, I'd like some peace.
If that's O.K. with You?

Just for a moment, is all I ask,
One moment of Your bliss,
Is that so hard to grant to me?
You could do it with a flick of your wrist.

But maybe I am mistaken,
Do You really care?
Maybe You're nowhere at all,
Maybe You're just not there.

Maybe You're on Vacation,
Pitching Your tent somewhere,
Or maybe You're just tired,
With the people way down here!

Maybe you've had Your fill,
Of the ant hill here below,
Maybe You'll just bury us,
Beneath a mound of snow.

Maybe You'll just forget us,
We're not what You had planned,
Maybe you thought Your creation,
Just got out of hand.

Maybe you thought we could handle all this,
I didn't know God could be deceived,
And even though I'm saying all this,
I still wish I could believe!

GOING PLACES

I took her down, on to the floor,
I love you, she said to me,
And I am sure one day, you'll be,
The ruler of the seven seas.

I looked at her for awhile.
And then I took her by her hand,
And then I asked her why it was
She couldn't accept me for" What I am?"

"But, darling, please;
Think on it,
You could make a plan,
If not the seven seas," said she,
"You could rule the land."

"Darling, please listen,
You don't understand,
I don't want to rule the sea,
Nor do I want to rule the land."

Ambition is a dangerous thing,
And your love is all I need,
Aren't you happy with me, dear?
Do I have to plead?"

"Well, if that's the way you feel,
You can take me home,
I have plans of another sort,"
And she left me all alone!

The moral of the story is,
And it is plain to see,
She wanted gold and silver;
I just wanted to be me!

CRAP AND CORRUPTION,
HELL AND DAMNATION

I'd like to write something soft,
Something sweet and gay,
Oh, crap! You can't use that term anymore!
The world just turned out that way!

I'd like to write something tender and gentle,
Something to soothe your ear,
Something to give you peace of mind,
But it's to late, I fear!

Something that would bring back your youth,
To bring back sweet memory,
Something to remind you of the good times,
It would mean the world to me!

Something that would bring back innocence,
Something to revive your soul,
Something to bring back all the joy,
That you once had, I know.

Something that would ease your constant
pain,
As you do grow old,
Something to cure your broken heart,
But it's too late, I'm told!

The hurricane is coming,
The driving wind is here,
The cloud is hanging above our heads,
The end, it does grow near!

Yes, I am dark! A pessimist!
There isn't much more to tell,
I hope we get to Heaven,
Before we get to Hell!

I DO!

If you don't show up tonight,
It's quits!
You don't know that by now,
But I do! I do!

If you don't carry through,
It's quits!
You don't know that now,
But I do! I do!

If you can't prove your love for me,
It's quits!
You don't know that now,
But I do! I do!

You've taken every thing I had,
All my money, and what's more,
You took away my heart, so sad,
And walked out of the door.

And if you don't know it by now,
All the pain that I've gone through,
I really wouldn't wish, not I,
The same; happening to you!

So, if you keep feeding me lies,
Excuse, after excuse, after excuse!
I'm going to leave you flat, and, Baby,
I'm telling you the truth.

You really don't know that by now,
But I do! I do! ......I do!!!!

I HOPE THAT I'M NOT WRONG

All the suffering in the world,
Plays upon my mind,
Like the gall that Jesus drank,
Like a bitter taste of wine.

How much longer, must we suffer?
Is there a way out?
I ponder it, and I am left,
With a lot of doubt.

The Price it has been paid, they say.
Then why do I feel the pain?
Why is that I hurt deep inside?
What is this pounding in my brain?

Why is it that I cry so much?
For my fellow man?
I really don't know how everything,
Got so out of hand!

Wars, guns, calamity,
Chaos in the street.
Drugs and murders, the toll is rising,
The starving children at our feet.

Is love and compassion truly gone?
Is there no mercy to be found?
Are we all like Cain? I ask myself
Destined to spill the blood of others
Upon this barren ground?

Jesus tried to teach us,
Did we listen? No!
So it seems to me
That we are doomed,
To a life below!

This I know, and it's true,
And a very hurtful song.
If we can change, our fate may too,
I hope that I'm not wrong!

*And because iniquity shall abound, the love of
many shall wax cold.*

Mathew 24:12

I NEED YOU, BABY!

Oh, my dear, Oh my dear,
You would not believe,
How fast I fell in love with you,
So please, do not deceive.

Oh, my dear, oh my dear,
I would not forget,
That beautiful bronze body,
By my side, in hopes of splendor; yet.

For I love you with all my heart,
My love I send to you.
On wings of Angels, on wings of doves,
For my love is true.

Now, so, you have it, my precious one
Plain and simple, too,
And I'm so lucky, Oh my dear
To be wanted by you.

And I need you,
Close to me,
By my aching side,
Be close to me, as I'm to you,
Forever, love will bide!

IS IT TOO LATE?

A basket with two fishes,
A basket, five loaves of bread,
Can feed five thousand,
That's what the Bible said!

And if a man asks you for his coat,
Give him your cloak, too;
And if a man asks you to go a league,
Remember, go with him two.

Love thy brother as thyself,
That is the golden rule.
But now people think only of themselves,
Hasn't the world grown cruel?

I think the age is upon us,
For men are lovers of themselves,
Disobedient and unthankful,
Boasters and truce breakers,
In corruption, they do delve!

And we are no better,
For the lessons we've been taught,
Has never produced any fruit,
Is it too late? I pray not!

IT REALLY DOESN'T MATTER

Free verse is the form I use,
It doesn't have to rhyme.
And the meter, it is out of place,
I have no sense of time,
Whoops!

It's just that I'm not comfortable,
With all those stupid rules,
I never learned them, anyway
Rules are just for, you know.

So, as I write, I'd like to think,
That I am a nonconformist,
But that doesn't mean I'm out of line,
It's all in the performance.

So if you like it, that is fine,
If you don't, well, that's fine too,
I really don't have anything,
I want to prove to you.

There I go, done it again,
Rhymed when I didn't mean to,
What the hell, all is well,
The crap we have to go through!

So, what is it that I am?
A poet or a shyster?
I don't know.
Can you tell me?
I learned it all,
From my T.V.!

So, it really doesn't matter!

JEZEBEL

Ah! Jezebel, I know your name,
Some call you Delilah, too.
That's not what you call yourself,
But other people do!
Whose arms are you in, tonight?
Promising them some more delight?
You're a shadow that is black as night,
And I, I still love you!

What promises did you give them?
That you will never fulfill?
What ecstasy did you give them
That keeps them at your will?
What Siren song do you sing,
That keeps them at your hem?
And I love you, and I love you still!
You're really quite a gem!

And me? I am just another fool,
Who was taken, taken in by you,
I should have known it from the start,
But they never taught this in school!

So all day long, I sit and cry,
What more is it, I can do?
I am surrounded by misery all the time,
And it's all because of you!

JOY AND MISERY

They say a clown that is full of laughter,
Is hiding misery inside.
And that every prank, and every trick,
There's a tear that he must hide.

And when the stage is empty,
And all the people have gone home,
He sits and weeps, for all he's worth
While he's sitting all alone.

And he knows tomorrow will be the same,
As he takes his make up off.
Aided by the tears that he has shed,
And it happens oft.

He steps outside to breathe the air,
That his heartaches took away.
He's waiting for another dawn,
Another break of day.

When the gates are to be opened,
To the crowd, that will be coming in,
Then he'll put a smile upon his face,
It's really quite a sin.

For the show, it must go on, you see.
There is no doubt about it.
Although the clown makes me joyful at times,
I can do without it!

And as much as it hurts me so,
This joy and misery,
This laughter and the cry.
The clown reminds me of someone I know,
Is it you and I?

JUDAS

I will never see Heaven's Gate,
Something I've done amiss!
I strolled into the Garden;
Jesus' cheek, to kiss!

And I will find a potter's field
Thirty pieces of silver to buy,
Then I'll burst my bowels asunder,
For now, I'll surely die!

Judas is my name.
That's all that must be done
The Son of Perdition,
Not the Prodigal Son!

Forever torture, flames of fire,
That is where I tread!
The guilt that I feel, brought me here,
To this place of dread!

No peace for me, for my betrayal,
All that's left is agony!
So foolish, was I, and in the end,
I suffer for eternity!

This is a warning, what I say is true.
Kiss the Son, but not like I did,
Lest, He be angry.
Don't let this happen to you!

JUST BEFORE YOU CALLED

I was doing fine,
Just before you called,
Now I realize,
I was once again,
Once again, stone walled!

Just not getting anywhere,
When it comes down to our love,
It's so sad, and I'm always blue,
It's not fair, my Dove.

I'm not getting any sleep,
I'm up all-night, again,
So aware of my constant pain,
And it is driving me insane!

You could have left me all alone,
I really should have been ignored,
Then, I wouldn't feel so bad,
My life is in such discord.

I really love you, way too much,
And much to my downfall,
I'm afraid, once you're through with me,
I won't feel any thing at all!

JUST DESERTS

I had an angry teacher once,
Her name was Miss McGhee,
Throughout all the year, I was in fear,
She had a pick on me.

I could not escape her.
No, no, not at all,
She had caught me one time,
I was innocently in the hall.

"Why are you not in class?"
Her eyes were fiery red!
"I just had to take a pee."
I had shyly said.

"Who gave you permission?
I know it wasn't me!"
"Was the fact I had to go,
Nature called, you see!"

"Because you have position,
Doesn't mean that you rule me!"
That's when I learned a lesson from,
That old crow, Miss McGhee

Slammed against the lockers,
Dragged down the corridor,
That's when I felt a rage,
I've never felt before.

With all my strength, I broke free,
I ran towards the door,
With Miss McGhee, chasing me,
"You won't catch me!" I swore.

Up the path, up to the cliff,
That over looked the shore,
With McGhee on my heels,
My legs were getting sore.

Suddenly, I heard a splash
McGhee, she had fallen in.
And then it occurred to me,
McGhee, she cannot swim!

SOME DAY

They say that time heals all wounds,
That misery must fade,
That sorrow will soon be gone,
Like the withered blade.

That God will wipe away all tears,
And fill us full of joy,
It just seems to take forever,
Or am I being coy?

Did I give up on God?
Or did He give up on me?
Is there an answer anywhere?
Where then, can that be?

There was an answer that I had,
When I was in my youth,
I was so bold and sure of it,
That I had found the truth!

The Straight Gate now, where is it?
It faded from my sight.
In danger now of Hell Fire.
To where there is no light!

LOST

I'm not drunk enough!
Can someone help me?
Just to ease the pain?
Because my darling wife,
God took her home
And I am lost, again!

LOVE

Shattered shells of souls,
And waves of tattered goals,
And the coloured pieces of love,
For which I long,
Turn into disillusionment,
Twisted girders,
And a partly written song.

WORRIED

I remember something said by someone,
"All your worrying, will not effect the sun!"
But, still, I cry!
Something is still missing,
Something in my brain,
I am still too human,
And not enough, humane!

ALONE

I am alone!
I, with no one to comfort me, am alone,
Alone, I was born, save for my mother,
And I am so small,
And must learn to stand tall,
I must not give into what I believe is wrong,
I must fight with my all,

Until death!

MISGUIDED LOVE CORRECTED

Oh, dear God, I want to call her!
Refrain, refrain, refrain!
Jesus, I long to speak to her!
Refrain, refrain, refrain!

Love is a golden light,
That will come to you again;
Just be patient, wait and see,
True love will ease the pain.

But, my Lord, don't you know,
Don't you understand?
The love I want is so far from me,
I can't even hold her hand!

I'm telling you this once,
Love is not that way,
Love is giving of yourself,
Every single day!

Love is not about yourself,
Sometimes Love is cruel.
Love is really about sacrifice,
Love is the Golden rule.

Love is about caring,

For your brother, who has gone astray!
Love is about sharing,
What more can I say?

And Love does not require a reward,
Love does not require pay.
Love is the gift from the heart,
Love is the only way.

Love is neither sex nor money,
Love is not things you get,
Love is sacrifice, my son,
Don't you know that yet?

And I sacrificed for all, you see,
For my fellow man.
Pick up your cross and follow me,
Salvation is at hand!

MORE MISERY THAN JOY

When the world has taken all from you,
And no peace can be found,
And you feel forsaken,
And friends don't come around,
And the enemy is at your doorstep,
And you just want to cry,
Think of others, who've lost more than you,
The ones that said goodbye.

The men that have been through a war,
The memories haunt them still,
The Martyrs that died in God's name,
Heaven's plan to fulfill,
The misguided ones that lost their way,
The people of the streets,
The ones who thought they'd never fall,
The ones that beg for meat.

This world is full of pain and strife,
Yes, that is very true.
Is there no way to heal the pain
That we all go through?
For it seems to me,
There's more misery than joy,
How I wish for innocence,
Back when I was a boy!

When sailing ships under a big vast sky,
Would glide upon the waves,
And tales of great heroes did abound,
And courage was displayed.
When people helped their fellow man,
When they were down and out.
When people knew what real love was,
And people had no doubt!

Or was this all a child's dream?
Never to be real?
A fantasy within my head,
Could people really feel
The love for one another?
When all were called your brother?
This world is just so damaged!
I pray God will build another.

But surely, if He does,
I hope He learned from His mistake.
That He will grant us brotherhood,
And banish all the hate!

MY DEAREST,

I can't shake you off my mind,
You're so sweet, and lovely,
And you are
So kind.

If I had a fortune,
And if I had some time,
I'm sure one day, for certain,
I could make you mine!

You know I would do anything,
If I could keep you dear,
But all I can offer is myself,
Not enough to keep you near.

Money, I don't have any,
And gold, I have none,
But I know that my love is true,
As sure as there is a sun.

So think of me, once in awhile,
Wherever you may be,
And I promise you,
I'll be thinking of you,
From here to Eternity.

MY MIND!

Why would you want to torture me?
You know that it's not right!
Promises you never keep
Keeps me awake at night!

Why is it that I sigh for you?
Because you're no good for me!
You are Danger, plain and simple
I've come to that reality!

A cheater and a liar,
When will you be true?
And, still I can't forget you,
I must be crazy, too!

There'll come a day, I will forget you,
Someday very soon,
For death is waiting at the door
I'm getting old so rapidly,
Such a familiar tune.

That's when I will forget you,
My casket, underground.
When I get judged for the wrongs I've done.
My judgments; so unsound!

But for now, all those memories,
Keep on haunting, on and on.
And in my mind, I'll see you.
Until my mind is gone!

MY WIFE

'Twas in the year 2009
The third month of the year,
That the Angles came, took my darling wife,
My lovely, lovely dear.

Now, I'm not angry with God,
Far be it from me,
But I just can't understand,
Why things like this must be.

Is there a plan, I ask myself?
The answer eludes me still,
For men to suffer all the time,
Is this His eternal will?

Is there peace in the heavens?
When we do go there?
But right now, where I am,
All I feel is fear.

Is there an answer to my question?
Is there an answer when we die?
For it seems all I do right now,
Is sit and wonder why.

So every thing's a cycle,
The wheels keep spinning round,
While we're still here, on this earth,
The answer won't be found.

And when we die, in the appointed time,
For now, life's so unfair.
If all our questions are answered then,
Will we even care?

NO CREATIVITY

I'm not feeling so creative today,
So I'm grasping for something clever to say.
I guess I may be boring you,
Please don't let me know that's true.

Maybe tomorrow, who does know,
I may say something profound and so,
Until tomorrow, we shall see,
What words of wisdom come out of me!

NOT I!

I am not a piece of clay;
You should have guessed that by now!
To be pushed and broken at the back
Just to make me bow!

I am not a puppet thing,
I need no-one to make me talk,
Or pull my strings, to make me walk
Or to tell me how to eat my jam,
I am exactly what I am!

I am not a button thing,
Won't be pushed to make me sing,
Won't be prodded to do your thing,
And if I should changed in any way,
It's my own will to leave or stay.

I am like water, in many ways,
I can change just like the tide,
It's the consequences, that do change,
And they are my only guide!
I am what I am, at the time that I am.
Hey you; I'm a man!

THE NUMBER GAME

One, Two Three, Four,
I'm looking for the exit door,
Five, six, seven, eight,
I'm bailing out, before it's too late,
Nine, ten, eleven, twelve,
I'm just an ornament on your shelf,
Thirteen, fourteen, fifteen, sixteen,
I'm jumping off your hook, don't make a
scene!
Seventeen, eighteen, nineteen, twenty,
Heartaches from you; I've had plenty,
Twenty-one, twenty-two, twenty-three,
twenty-four,
I don't love you anymore!

OH, VALIANT HEARTS

Oh, valiant hearts of days gone by,
You fought for what you believed,
Making war, against the foe,
In strength, valor and deed,
What has become of your lives?
Laid wasted for God and king,
On steeds of white,
You went to fight,
But what good did it bring?
The world is as it was before,
Oh, valiant hearts of days gone by,
Stick your bloody wars!

Oh, gentle hearts of days gone by,
Still weeping for your men,
Give them up, Oh, give them up,
They won't return again!
All day long, you sit and cry,
For the men that you have lost,
You're getting old, but you were told,
To hang on to your cross.
Weep, weep, oh, gentle hearts,
Fill the sea with tears,
For 'tis said this foolishness,
Must needs go on for years.

Oh, gentle hearts of days to come,
Get on with your chores,
Oh valiant hearts of days to come,
Stick your bloody wars!

ONE AND ONE AND ONE = NONE
(Youth)

A had a friend who dropped by
To my house; one day,
He had a friend,
A Charming lass,
To her, I had to say,
"Will you be mine
My pretty one?'
A kiss or two did pass,
With that, and what we've done before
She had answered "Yes."

In seventh heaven, that I was!
A delightful little girl,
She filled me with so much confidence,
I could beat the world.
Then one day, by happenstance
There she was, as bold as brass,
My friend was there, too
The truth was out at last!

One and one and one are two,
This is something I never knew,
'Til one day, as I walked along
I had seen two love birds sing their song.

My heart was broken,
How could that be?
So I waited for an opportunity,
To question her about her love,
And then she softly said to me,
"I love you with all my heart,
It's just you and me."
And so I prayed to God above.
To the Power that must be!

I confronted her with the facts I knew.
I declared it plain and simple,
"It's either him or I" I said to her,
"So now you have to choose!"
"To put me in that position," she said,
"It is really not quite so fair,
I love him, but I love you, too!"
And then she left us both standing there!

PAIN

You are like a dream that comes and goes,
Filling me with strife,
You appear, and then disappear;
I need substance in my life!

You are like the changing winds,
Never know from which way you come,
Ever changing, never staying,
Never one place for too long.

I don't think I can handle this,
Never one place, never home,
Always waiting, always waiting,
For you to become my own.

Is it too much to ask of you,
For a moment of peace and serenity?
For I love you, I'll love you always,
But, this pain; it is killing me!

PRECIOUS

Spill the coffee,
Spill the tea,
Spill the wine,
Won't be happy,
Until you're here with me!

Take my love,
For what it is!
I'm forever true,
Won't cause you pain,
Won't cause you grief,
I really do love you!

So, come on home,
My pretty One,
Come be by my side!
Forever, and forever,
I will make you,
My lovely, lovely bride.

That is if you'll have me,
That is if you'll stay,
Don't let me down,
Don't let me down,
Be with me for always!

I'll shout it to the wind,
I'll shout it to the sea,
In all the world,
My precious one,
There's only you and me!

PRODUCTION

Production, Production,
Keep on rolling
Keep it coming fast.
Get it in there,
Get it going,
Make sure you're not last!

Don't take your time,
'Cause time is money
There's a deadline to be met.
Keep it moving!
Keep improving,
You haven't made it yet,

"Can't we just slow down the pace?"
"No, by God, it is a race!
Can't you just realize,
The first one in, will win a prize?"

Monetary gain is an achievement,
To hell with love, and all that buzz!
Just look forward to your next reward,
Fill up the coffers, my dear Cuz.

Be satisfied, with all the wealth,
Never mind the consequence,
Being poor is not an option,
Being poor, it makes no sense!

Filthy lucre, is no solution,
Causes strife for you and me,
Ungodly gain is a delusion,
Why then, can't you see?
Money alone can't buy you love,
Neither health, nor contentment,
Money alone can't set you free!
It will make you subservient!

So let us reason together,
In the end, I hope you'll see;
That love of money, is just a snare,
A trap for you and me,

QUESTIONS

Is Heaven a place, or a state of mind?
Is Heaven a plane or a space in time?
I know the question is quite insane
But does mind even require a brain?

If a mind does not require a brain
Then it can live on forever.
Then, surely Heaven can exist
It can die…. Not ever!!!!!

So what is the answer that I seek?
What is the question, I propose?
Life, Eternity, Peace, Serenity,
Can they be found? I do suppose.

The answer lies within the heart
The answer lies way up Above
The only answer that there is,
Is God's eternal LOVE!

SAD, ISN'T IT?

There is a man that I know,
Or should I say, a child,
He hasn't grown up, not one bit,
His parents made him wild.

He has a nasty habit,
This is all that he can do,
Is pull a prank that isn't funny,
On everyone; me and you.

He makes fun of people,
That's his style
But every one can see,
The poor lad is destined for,
A full lobotomy!

Oops, I think I should take that back,
I think I made a blunder,
The lobotomy must have already been done,
It's time to take him under!

IS IT SOMETHING IN MY PROFILE?

Is it something in my profile,
Something that I missed,
Or is it that I have such a,
Such a sloppy kiss?

It's not my looks,
For I am handsome,
In an ugly way,
And I am not talented,
That's for sure;
What more can I say!

Maybe I'm cross eyed,
Bowlegged, maybe, too.
Maybe the mirror lies to me
I'm not seeing what is true!
Maybe I'll have another drink.
I'm toasting it to you!

SORROW

Did I just have a vision?
A woman sweet, but so unreal.
A delusion, perhaps, a fallacy,
Please, Lord, hear my appeal"

Did I have a vision
In the dark of night?
Did I hear in the waves a 'murmur?
Did I see a light?

Did I go to sleep at all?
Am I still awake?
Was there a comforting sound?
Or was it a mistake?

Did I hear some laughter?
Children full of joy?
Did I go back to my youth?
Am I still a boy?

Age is a state of mind,
Or so I heard them say,
And growing old, all alone,
Is at the end of day.

We came in this world, a pauper,
And we'll take nothing when we go,
All is gloom, to those above,
As we settle six feet below.

I played my part on the stage,
My lines weren't always right,
There were many a time I stumbled,
Groping through the night.

Is there any end of this?
This carousel of life?
I'm in despair, for I miss,
My Love, my Dove, my wife!

SPRING

Spring is here, at last,
To sweep away the gloom.
The sky is bright, The birds do sing,
The flowers are in bloom!

The gentle wind from the bay;
The smell of the salt filled air.
The sunshine brings us gladness,
And takes away despair.

Put on your light clothes,
Go for a hike,
Go for a ride
Upon your bike!

All your cares, throw them away,
Leave all your worries behind.
Talk with people on the way,
I'm sure they will not mind.

The sun now is descending,
Just below the hill.
The rays of light play on the clouds,
The wind, it has gone still.

You can hear the rustling in the bush,
The squirrel chatters away.
Time for you to go home.
It is the end of day.

You settle in the rocking chair,
That's nested on your porch.
Sweet thoughts of the day come to mind,
As you light the backyard torch.

Yes life is great and beautiful,
You haven't got a care.
And it would be nice if spring would stay,
Throughout the entire year!

STILL MISSING HER!

A year has past, and I'm still weeping,
For my darling wife, in God's arms is sleeping.
I saw her last night, in a dream,
She looked so kind and fair,
But when I awoke, with the dawn,
Again she wasn't there!

God, I miss her! Can't you see
That I'm in so much despair?
I wish that I could hold her now,
But again, she isn't here.

Life is so sad, at the best of times,
Life sometimes seems so unkind,
I wish for her so, constantly,
She's forever in my mind.

Although I know, I must move on,
And the heartache, it must go.
Deep inside, she's always there,
Ever haunting me, I know.

So if I ever meet a lover in my old age,
That would love me, and always true,
She'll have to be satisfied,
That I love another, too!

SUFFERING

I am feeling so miserable,
You can plainly tell.
My life is nothing but heartache,
My tears begin to well.

Sorrow comes and grips my heart,
Each and every day,
Isn't there anything better?
For that, I always pray.

What chance does a man have,
In this world of pain?
Where do we go from here?
I'm asking, once again.

Strife and confusion, it does abound
Every where you look,
Abductions and murder, all around,
One could write a book.

Oh, Gabrielle, Oh Gabrielle,
When will you sound your horn?
And take us to our Savior,
For we are so forlorn!

Lost, lost in this sea of sin,
When will it leave our hearts?
And when Christ comes, will we be ready?
Or be stranded in the Dark?

TARJA

For all the laughter,
For all the tears,
For loving you,
All these years.

I never thought that it would end,
I never thought that we would part
It didn't even cross my mind,
I'd have this broken heart.

May Jesus wrap you in His arms,
As He carries you away,
And to your Heavenly Father,
For this, my love, 1 pray.

And Joy and Peace, they say that's there,
But here, I cannot find,
But I promise to you, my sweet, sweet dear:
I'll see you in due time.

And the things that I said to you,
About being good before you went,
I believed them when I said them,
But my world had gotten bent.

And hopefully, I'll find again,
The path that will lead to you,
For in all this world, and the One you're in,
Your love was always true.

My Darling, I miss you!

In loving memory of my wife, Tarja,
who passed away on March 22, 2009.

TARJA, MY LOVE

Watching those old monitors,
In the hospital,
Something tells me, it's for sure,
That nothing's going well!

I knew it that morning, it was her final time.
I knew it. I knew it, I knew it; I knew it in my
mind,
But I could not seem to tell her that,
This was the fateful kind!

And I do still love her,
Although she has gone away,
I could have told her, this was the end,
It seemed so pointless to say,

Why should I have added to her misery?
I'm sure she knew anyway,
She lovingly patted me on my arm
Before she passed away

Just to say I love you,
Just to say farewell,
She is bound for Heaven
For me? I cannot tell!

TECHNOLOGY

In this world of enchantment,
Man has made an advancement,
Tearing down trees to build up homes,
Scientific ways to date back bones,
Better ways for man to think,
Someone's looking for the missing link,
The U.S. and Russia are having a race,
To see who can put the best junk up into space,
They're trying to invent an inflatable balloon,
That if blown big enough, will whistle a tune,
Bigger and better bombs, oh what fun!
They're harnessing the energy from the sun,
And everyone here thinks it is very swell,
But I have a feeling,
I have a feeling,
I have a feeling,
We're headed for Hell!

TIME

Time, with its mighty fist and tremendous
force,
Has always shaken the very foundations of my
dreams,
And I wake up in the morning,
To the sounds of piercing screams.

UNREQUITED LOVE

Every day, I sigh,
And every night I cry,
And all the spare times in between,
Are only lousy dreams

THAT NIGHT

'When will Jesus come back?' she asked me,
Well he came back for her that night,
And Jesus wasn't so kind to me,
I lost my guiding light.

I was never one to doubt my God,
I thought I would always believe,
But things have changed, since that night,
Seems all I do is grieve!

The Flower that bloomed every morn,
The Angel, that she was,
Is a heartache now, because she's gone,
My eternal Love.

Always forgiving, that she was,
Forgiveness I didn't deserve,
I loved my precious baby with all my breath,
But life threw me a curve.

Am I to blame for believing?
I read her letters through and through,
I will love you forever, forever, she wrote.
I hope that's really true!

For I'll love her until the day I die,

And my soul begs to depart,
This messed up world, and all it's suffering,
Just to ease my aching heart.

Here I am, all alone,
Just waiting for that day,
If God would only be so kind,
To take my hurt away.

Someday on that immortal shore,
We may meet again,
Forever, Baby, I love you,
But for now, I'm still in pain!

THE CREATURE

Feel the flame that drowns the night,
And opens up the mind,
To touch eternity,
Seek peace and serenity,
To see the people of this land,
Ever seeking, with the question,
Am I, or not, a man?

Burning embers pass our eyes,
Falling to the sand,
Striking with a purple light,
The powers of mankind.
And in the pit, the Creature stands,
Stupefied, with open mouth,
Staring at the gap he had placed,
Between him and himself!

MY DREAMS

My dreams are of a far off land,
A few do tread with me,
I hear the sound of the whispering wind,
And the sound of the crashing sea,
Where ships they have no captains,
And every one is free,
Where loosened bonds,
And love of life,
Makes friends out of enemies

THE SEDUCTION

I'm searching for love.
That eternal flame,
I don't need fortune
I don't need fame,

Looking for that perfect thing
Is a concept I reject
For looking for perfection,
Can lead you to regret,

I've looked for perfection,
I've looked for it, long and far,
But inlaid gold and silver
Would not be found in tar.

So, love is all I ask of you,
If you can give it, free,
I won't ask that much of you,
So, don't ask that much of me!

Although, I need some comfort,
In my final days,
Just be here, my pretty one,
And while the time away!

For if I was a perfect man,
Perfection, I'd prefer,
But don't worry any; I'm not that kind,
And you're not, I am sure.

So come on little darling,
I have something to confess
I told you I was a Bohemian
I'm not a Hedonist!
So come on, baby, take my hand,
I'll gaze into your eyes,
And I'll love you forever,
If you'll just compromise!

THE SERVANT IS NOT
ABOVE HIS MASTER

Sitting in the sunlight,
On a cloudless day,
Wondering if my troubles,
Will ever go away?

Stayed here 'til the day was past,
Now stars are in the sky,
Without you; my precious love,
And still, I wonder why?

God, in His infinite wisdom,
Took you away from me.
He must have a plan, or so, I wish,
But, that, I cannot see.

The trees are still green,
The sky, it is still blue,
Life goes on, I'll carry on
But, alas, without you!

So someone,
Can you tell me please?
While I'm still here,
On my knees.

While I am here, so sad and blue,
In my little crazy world;
Is it that you have suffered too?
Are the Angels wings unfurled?

So, in the end, so plain to see,
Despite my endless misery,
Christ suffered, too, for you and me,
To take us to Eternity!

THE WOLF

I will hunt with no weapons,
Save for my craft, in this hinterland,
I live as the animals live,
I hate the smell of man.

I have seen men grow fat,
Off of other men's work,
I've seen the women rise above the men,
Now softened by the fork.

The only companion that I want,
Is one that will hunt with me,
And the only blood dripping from our
mouths,
Will be that of necessity!

TOUGH TIMES

My memories of long ago,
When the cracks in the wall
Would let in the snow,
And I remember long before,
When ice would form upon the floor

When the stove gave up,
There was no heat!
Hardly any thing to eat,
Shoveled coal that would not light,
The coal, it was too wet,
The good times when all was bad,
How could I ever forget?

When I was going off to school,
No breakfast on that morn,
No lunch money in our pockets,
My clothes dirty and torn,

And all the children would laugh at us,
And call us awful names,
And after school, when we got home,
It seemed, nothing had changed!

I remember finding a quarter
On the neighbour's stoop,
I gave it to my grandmother,
For her bowl of soup!

Going to the outhouse,
In three feet of snow,
I was only four foot two,
It was a hard, hard go!

TORTURE

Every moment that passes by,
For every second on the clock,
Minute by minute, hour by hour,
Every agonizing tick, tick, tock;
I sit and wonder why.

Every sound that I hear,
Every car that rushes by,
Hour on hour, day by day,
I wonder why, I wonder why;
I wonder why you're not here.

So now, it has come to this,
For every moment you are here,
Second upon second, minute by minute,
My enchanting, beautiful dear;
It is eternal bliss.

Every heartbeat, every breath I breathe
Every sigh that I do take,
Every fear, every tear,
I feel my body shake;
For fear that you may leave.

I love every hand hold, every hug,
And every lovely kiss;
But, every time you go away;
Love shouldn't hurt like this !

WAS IT A MISTAKE?

I've waited for a few days now,
for the reply to my mail.
And I don't know what is going
on; my reason seems to fail,
I'm thinking that I lost you,
as a valued friend,
I hate that that should happen,
didn't mean to offend!

To tell the truth, I don't
regret, every little kiss,
I don't regret holding you,
I felt some tenderness.
I don't regret seeing you;
I missed your little smile.
I don't regret wanting you,
even for a while.

What I regret is that I'm not,
the man that I should be!
That I gave in to wanting,
as you can plainly see,
I guess I'm like all the rest,
what a shock to me!
I guess it's true what has been said,
I'm my own worst enemy!

I have my troubles, quite a few,
That I must address.
Please, can't you forgive me?
I can't stand the stress!

Now you say you want me,
Only as a friend.
I'll accept that, if that's the case.
But, who, really can foresee,
What is in the end?

WHAT NOW?

The Chardonnay was Blah!
But the Cabernet was fine,
But what the heck do I know?
I'm not a connoisseur of wine!

All I know is what I like,
What makes me feel so good,
What makes me feel so well inside,
But it's not my neighborhood.

The people that you see each day,
As they go passing by,
With a nod, or with a phony smile,
With an unconcerned "Hi"

Don't they know the world will crumble?
That the world comes to an end?
That the only hope for us all,
Is if we love our fellow man?

But maybe I'm too optimistic,
Maybe I've been fooled.
War and hate, it does abound,
Not the golden rule!

"Love your neighbour as yourself",
Is what I've often heard.
And I was told, by a chosen few,
These words came from Our Lord.

Are we so stupid,?
Are we that blind?
Are we in denial?
I'm afraid there's no hope now,
To guarantee our survival!

WHERE DID OUR LOVE GO?

Where did our love go?
Where, oh where?
We lost a rainbow,
There's something,
Missing here!

Come out and see me,
Dear, oh dear,
We can make it!
I still care: don't you?

I love you,
You love me too,
I'm really sorry for,
The way I've treated you.

Oh, my love, I'll change,
I swear, I'll be true,
There isn't anything,
I wouldn't do; for you.

I've been searching
All of my life,
But, you're the only one,
I want for my wife.

Where did our love go?
Oh where, oh where?
We lost a rainbow,
There's something,
Missing here!

Missing here!

YOU CAN'T FOOL ME

Out of the heart, the mouth speakest.
So quiet, be thy tongue!
Unless you want to prove to the world,
That you have been among,

The savage kind, the cripplers,
The murderers and thieves,
The hustlers and the con artists,
From which the people have no relief.

The cowards and the fly by nights,
And people that deal drugs,
The people that beat you just for kicks,
The people that cannot love.

The people that will chain you up,
With no conscience nor pity, too,
That torture and mistreat you,
They will kill you through and through!

And what was it you said, my dear,
When you were all astir?
I'll be coming back, But not with you!
This, you harshly swore!

But then you took it back.,
That is not what you meant.
It was the passion of the moment,
When you were badly bent.

But I know deep down inside,
When you do come here,
It won't be long until you're gone
To the life that you hold dear.

To the savage kind, the cripplers,
The murderers and the thieves,
The hustlers and the con artists
Of whom you are the chief!